THE LIFE OF ANTHONY

(Abridged)

BY SAINT ATHANASIUS

SAINT SHENOUDA PRESS

THE LIFE OF ANTHONY

(Abridged)

BY SAINT ATHANASIUS

WITH CONTEMPLATION BY
POPE SHENOUDA III

ST SHENOUDA PRESS
SYDNEY, AUSTRALIA
2020

THE LIFE OF ANTHONY

St Athanasius

WITH CONTEMPLATION BY

Pope Shenouda III

ST SHENOUDA PRESS
8419 Putty Rd,
Putty, NSW, 2330
Sydney, Australia

www.stshenoudapress.com

ISBN 13: 978-0-6488658-0-3

Contents

The Life of St Anthony   9

Contemplations by Pope Shenouda III   49

Our Love and Veneration of the Saints   53

St Anthony Strived and Triumphed   59

St Anthony as a Pioneer for
a New Spiritual System   65

St Anthony as a Teacher and Student   71

Did St Anthony give or take?   85

St Anthony and the Love of Solitude   95

St Anthony and the Love of God   101

Publisher's Note

St Anthony the Great, the 'Father of Monasticism', never opened a monastery himself, but St Athanasius says of him, "For monks, the life of Anthony is a sufficient example of asceticism."

Born in Egypt, and author of some of the earliest examples of monastic literature, St Anthony has been influential across the world, from the East to the West. To this day his life stands as a testimony to the ascetical life, which was both then and now, "spoken of everywhere, and admired by everyone."

In this book we have included an **abridged** version of the Greek translation of the Life of Anthony by St Athanasius, which we have endeavoured to make accessible for younger readers. Following this, we have included special contemplations by Pope Shenouda III on the life of St Anthony, who was a very special companion of His Holiness, who was originally named Fr Antonios as a monk.

We hope you find this edition eye-opening to the wonder of St Anthony's life and to the mysteries of asceticism.

The Life of St Anthony
By St Athanasius

Let us begin the history and life of the blessed St Anthony, as composed by St Athanasius, Archbishop of Alexandria. Through constant meditation on the following stories, your mind will be drawn to perfection through the example of this saint's works and deeds.

The Earliest Days

The blessed St Anthony was an Egyptian from a noble family. From his earliest childhood, he was brought up in the fear of the Lord. He was exceedingly modest and honest beyond measure. He was a simple man and a dweller of the tents. He never neglected any seasons of the Church, either in his childhood or early manhood.

When St Anthony was about twenty years old, his parents departed from the world and he was left alone with his sister. He was responsible for taking care of his sister. One day, while he was at church, a righteous idea entered his mind. He was mediating about how the blessed Apostles forsook everything and followed Christ. While he was meditating on this, the Holy Gospel was being read. He heard the words of our Lord who said: "If you wish to be perfect, go and sell everything you have, give to the poor, take up your cross and come after Me."

The blessed Anthony received the word of the Gospel as a sign to himself. It could not be by chance. Straightaway he went out of the church, departed to his house to sell all the possessions which he had inherited from his parents. He had 300 fields and a great estate which produced abundant crops. These he handed over to the people of his village. He distributed the rest of his possessions to the poor and kept a little which was sufficient for his sister's wants.

On another Sunday, he again entered the church and inclined his ear to the listening of the Gospel. As he inclined his ear, the Gospel read: "Take no thought for the morrow." Straight away he received the commandment readily. He spoke to his sister words of love, truth and fear of God and delivered her over to certain chaste nuns. He immediately became a solitary monk and he took no care for anything except his soul. He began to train himself in the habits of the strictest abstinence and self-denial. He dwelt alone in a house which was by the side of the village, for there were no monasteries for ascetics in Egypt at that time.

Answering the Call

Anthony was in constant meditation. He used to ponder within himself and say, "How did the righteous men of old live? With what manner did they please God?" Anthony's thoughts were exceedingly well disciplined from the beginning of his life of righteousness. He tried not to be anxious about his family, or fettered by the love of kinsfolk, or be held fast by the affairs of this temporary life.

He purged himself that he might be a pure offering to God. He used to labor with his hands, because he had heard the words, "If a man does not work, he shall not eat." He used to provide himself with food, and the rest he spent upon the poor. He prayed continually, for he had heard the words, "Pray, and let it not be tedious to you." He listened to the reading of the Scriptures in such a way that not one word might fall to the ground. He kept in his mind the remembrance of the commandments. Through these acts and deeds, the blessed Anthony "found favour with God and with man."

THE START OF TEMPTATION

Saint Anthony was the storehouse of fasting, prayer, ascetic labors, patient endurance and righteousness. When the enemy, the hater of the virtues and the lover of evil things, saw this great perfection in the young man, he could not endure it. The devil surrounded himself with his slaves and began to work on Anthony.

At the beginning, the devil approached Anthony with flattery. He cast him into anxiety for his possessions and sister. He tempted him with love of money and lusts of various kinds. He tempted him with thoughts so that by one thought the saint may be flattered or fall into the net of demonic instigation. Yet the more the enemy tempted St Anthony, the more strenuous the saint was in protecting himself with the armour of righteousness. The more the devil brought filthy and maddening thoughts, the more the saint took refuge in prayer and abundant supplication.

The devil used to appear to St Anthony in the form of a woman to burn him with lust. The blessed Anthony would kneel on his knees and pray: "O my Lord, I entreat You: do not let Your love be blotted out from my mind, and behold, I am, by Your grace, innocent before You." In all these things our Lord was his helper. He strengthened him to become a shield against the devil. Saint Anthony would say: "It was not I who worked, but Christ's grace which was with me."

When the enemy saw that he was vanquished in this fight against the saint, he gnashed his teeth. He appeared to Saint Anthony in the form of an Indian boy, and began to say to him, "I have come to overcome you." Whilst he was saying these words, the blessed Anthony made the Sign of the Cross and ceased to tremble. The Enemy saw the Sign of the Cross and was terrified. When the blessed Anthony saw that he was terrified, he began to ask him a question, saying, "Who are you?" The enemy said: I am the lover of error and fornication, and it is I who cast provoking thoughts and flatteries into the mind of man. I fight against every man and am against righteousness. It is I who injured you on several occasions, and you have been held in contempt by me in everything."

The blessed Anthony gave thanks to the Lord, and gained great encouragement, saying:

"What power do you think you have against the power of the Cross? I do not tremble at your wiles for the Lord helps me and I shall look in triumph upon my enemies." After hearing these words, straightaway the enemy vanished.

Although the blessed Anthony saw the enemy made powerless and brought low, he never neglected his prayers because he knew he was in war with a crafty being. He knew the Enemy was a roaring lion seeking whom he may devour. The saint knew that the snares of the Adversary were many so he contended strenuously in the fear of God.

The Seeking of Virtue

St Anthony kept vigil to the extreme, to such an extent that many days would dawn on him, without him getting any sleep. He was accustomed to eat in the evening but on some occasions he would go 3-4 days without eating. His food was bread and salt while his drink was water. He slept on a mat made of palm leaves but many times, the bare ground was his bed. He never pondered on how far he had advanced in his discipleship. He always said to himself: "A monk should know that in his manner of life he must be an alien to the world and an associate of angelic watchers."

The Struggle in the Tomb

After these things, St Anthony decided to leave the village and to take abode in a tomb cemetery. The tomb was situated in a mountain near the village. He commanded one of his acquaintances to bring him a morsel of bread from time to time. Having done these things, he entered the tomb and shut the door upon himself. Straightway the Adversary, together with a multitude of devils, burst upon him saying: "How great is that which you endure! To what limit will you drive yourself? You have now entered into the place of our abode. What man is there who has ever done this? When was it ever heard that men ought to live among the tombs? Therefore we will take vengeance upon you, for it is you who have made us fools."

The devil began to smite him with blows. They smote him so severely that he fell to the ground. Nothing but his breath was left in him. God helped him and would not deliver him over to death. His acquaintance would come to the tomb as he was accustomed to bring food. He would see the blessed Anthony almost dead, due to these blows. Straightaway, he would lift him up and bring him to the village church. With rest, the blessed saint would be refreshed, relieved from his affliction and would come to himself. He would then ask his acquaintance to take him back to the tomb. Sometimes St Anthony would have no power to stand up, that he would lie down and pray: "Where are you, O children of Gehenna? Although you multiply tortures, I shall not be remote from the love of Christ." Then he would say with a loud voice, "Though a whole legion of devils encamps against me, my heart shall not fear." These were the words which this saint proclaimed in his striving.

The heart of the Enemy melted within him. He would say to his associate devils: "What shall we do to this man who treats us with contempt and disdain? His heart is not afraid of quaking terror, his hearing is not perturbed by voices, his eyes are not terrified by visions and his body has no fear of blows. What else can be done to him?" The devils then contrived the following plan.

The devils caused a phantom earthquake which tore apart the four corners of the saint's house and they entered from all sides. One devil had the form of a lion, another the appearance of a wolf, another a panther and the others were in the forms of serpents, vipers and scorpions. The lion was roaring as though it was about to slay; the panther was prepared to spring upon him; and the snakes and vipers were hissing. The blessed Anthony was not disturbed or frightened by their commotion. His mind remained wholly undisturbed. As he was lying down, he laughed at these phantoms and said, "There is no power in you. You have taken the form of many wild beasts and you have lain plots and snares. My Lord is with me so your wickedness has no strength. If you are unable to do anything, why do you weary yourself in vain. My faith is a seal and a wall to me."

The Lord appeared to St Anthony after his

victory. St Anthony lifted his eyes and found a ray of light descending upon him. The devils dispersed in terror and the Lord came with consolation. St Anthony said: "O my Lord, I adore Your help. Where were You before these sufferings and tribulations came upon me?" Straightaway a voice came to him, saying, "I was by your side. I have never left you. I saw your strife and that you have overcome triumphantly. I will be your Guide and Comforter. I will make you renowned as a faithful servant throughout all the earth."

When St Anthony heard these words, he was filled with peace and rested from his afflictions. He rose up, bowed the knee, prayed and gave thanks to God Who had visited him. At that time Anthony was about thirty five years of age.

INTO THE DESERT

The following morning, the saint departed from the tomb and went to see a solitary old monk who used to dwell by the side of the village. The saint tried to persuade the old monk to go with him to the desert but the old monk excused himself from this. For one thing, it was his age. For the other, he was not accustomed to life in the desert. The saint then decided to head alone into the desert.

Once again, the enemy went after him. The devil showed the saint some gold and it was real gold. The blessed saint was not overthrown by it as he esteemed the gold as filth. St Anthony said to the devil: "Choose some other kind of handiwork and snare, for out of this one I have delivered myself." When the devil saw that St Anthony had protected himself with the sign of the Cross, he turned into a flame of fire.

The saint continued on the road he had been travelling. Having arrived into the desert, he went into a mountain where there were serpents. He continued to the bank of a river where he took his abode there. The saint shut himself and brought a supply of bread once every six months. The Egyptians at the time were in the habit of making bread to last that long. As for water, he found it there. He dwelt amongst the rocks, seeing no man and being seen by no one.

Sometimes people would come visit St Anthony but they would not be allowed to meet him in person. They would remain far and strain their ears. Many times they heard confusing sounds and cries of lamentation. Sounds of men at war or mighty tumults. Among this was a voice that said: "Depart from us! Why have you come to our country to cause our death? Have you ever heard that which your Lord spoke concerning us, saying, 'Evil spirits dwell in the desert, and in desolate places?' Behold, from now on you shall know that this is our habitation; depart you, and give place to us once more." These voices were that of the devil, waging war against the saint. The saint grew very courageous with every time the enemy was vanquished.

THE FAME OF THE HOLY MAN

When the report reached the city that St Anthony was fighting against devils, many other people decided to go visit him. As they approached the habitat of the saint, they heard a voice of one playing the harp and saying: "Let God arise, and let all His enemies be scattered. Let all those who hate Him flee before Him; let them be destroyed, even as smoke is made to disappear, and as wax melts before the fire, let the wicked perish before God. Again, all the nations compassed me round about, and in the Name of the Lord I destroyed them." The blessed Anthony lived in this habitation for twenty years.

It came to pass that in the process of time, the fame of St Anthony reached all the monks who were in Egypt. Monks began to visit him in large numbers. The Egyptian monks came that they might copy the manner of his life and deeds while the laity came that he might pray over them and might heal certain illnesses.

One day, a multitude of people came in a large group to see St Anthony. They begged him repeatedly to speak to him. They threw themselves down on their faces before him and they each made supplication before him. When he saw a large concourse of people, he was not disturbed. When they brought their petitions to him, he was not moved to impatient anger, but he remained in a placid and thoughtful state. Among those who came to him, there were many who were indeed very sorely afflicted, and our Lord healed them by the hand of St Anthony. Moreover, God gave him such a measure of grace in his speech that every man was wholly gratified. Those who were in affliction and distress were encouraged to endure. Those who were occupied with contention were quieted. Those who were afflicted sorely became long-suffering. The haughty were made humble and the arrogant were brought low.

St Anthony used to say, "We should not esteem anything of value besides the love of Christ, neither possessions nor kinsfolk, not even our soul itself." By these words he used to persuade many to withdraw themselves from this world, and from its tribulation, and to take refuge in a habitation of monks.

A Word from Athanasius on Perseverance

St Anthony began to increase in simple mindedness, in love towards strangers and in longsuffering. Let us continue to be strenuous and not become weary for our Lord is a Guide to us. The blessed Paul became an example by saying: "I die daily." If we were to think each day that we were to die that day, we will never sin at all. If it is morning, we should imagine that we will never make it to the evening. In this manner, we will never sin.

If we were to prepare our mind in this manner, and to live with this thought, we will never be overcome by sin. The lust which is fleeting would not reign over us. We will not love the possessions which pass away and we will forgive every man who offended us. The lust for women would die in the heart, for how could it be ministered?

Therefore, my beloved, let us be zealous in carrying out the work to which we have once bound ourselves, and let us travel to the end of the road on which we have begun to journey. Let no man look behind him, lest we be like the wife of Lot. He that turns back will repent of what he has done. Do not be afraid as if you were carrying a heavy burden, for the burden of our Lord is easy and light. If therefore we have the desire, everything is easy to us.

Joshua, the son of Nun, commanded the people, saying, "Prepare your hearts before the God of Israel," and John also said, "Prepare your ways." Therefore, take heed, my beloved sons, that you do not keep silent like those who have been brought low through sin or wrath or lust. For it is written lust conceives and brings forth sin, and when sin has been performed completely, it brings forth death. In this way, O my beloved, let us lead the life of watchfulness and strenuousness, as it is written, "Keep your heart with all diligence." We have cunning and crafty enemies and it is against these that our strife must be. The Apostle says: "Our contending is not against flesh and blood, but against principalities and powers, and against those who are masters of the world of darkness, which is beneath the heavens." Their contending against us is very frequent, and there is no rest from their attacks upon us.

ATHANASIUS UNCOVERS THE METHODS OF THE DEVIL

The whole race of devils is beyond measure an envious one. They are altogether jealous of mankind and particularly of the monks, for they cannot bear to see heavenly deeds wrought and heavenly lives led upon the earth. They, therefore, make hidden pits and snares for us, as it is written, "They have laid their nets over my paths." The word their "nets" means thoughts of iniquity. Let us not be afraid of their stirrings and let us not be made lax by reason of their flatteries. Instead, let us be constant in fasting and prayer, and straightaway they shall be vanquished and disappear.

We should not be terrified by the various species of devils or by the various forms they take. We should not be afraid of their voices, which are angry and threatening. The devil is a liar and there is no truth in his works or deeds. Although sin lifted up its horn, our Lord broke its sting. Sin is now beneath our feet and a laughing-stock to the nations. The devils are cunning, but they can only lead astray those who surrender to their powers.

Therefore, let us arm ourselves with the armour of righteousness and let us put on the helmet of redemption, and in the time of contending, let us shoot spiritual arrows from a bow which is stretched. The devils try to shout and wrangle and make tumultuous noises and commotions, that, perhaps, by means of sheer fright they may lead away weak minds. Yet the strength of the devil is nothing under the might of the Cross.

In what way can we increase our fear of God? Or in what way are we able to add to our contempt for the evil ones? Whenever we make our life and deeds better than they were before, we increase the pleasure we give to God, and we also multiply the contempt, which we have for the evil ones. The devils are afraid of a monk's fasting, prayers, chastity, abstinence, meekness and gentleness. These virtues pierce them on every side. It causes them anger and to foam at the mouth, thus the devil does anything it can to stop the monk.

You must distinguish between the things of the Holy Spirit and the things of the Evil one. How are we to make this distinction? First, you must pray and make supplication so that Christ, who is the Revealer of secrets, may give you this power. After prayer, comes experience. The visions and revelations of the Holy Spirit are not of a terrifying or tumultuous charmer. Rather they bring peace and tranquility. They have a gentle and quiet satisfaction to them.

On the other hand, the fright of the Evil one brings disturbance to the soul. The mind hears voices of great tumult. The timid soul becomes afraid. Life becomes full of tribulation and misery. Voices of drunken men and caves of robbers. Despite the crafts of the Evil one, let us not be moved by fear but let us stand bold and say with Jesus: "Get behind me Satan."

The Triumphs of Saint Anthony

On one occasion, the devils were found filling the saint's house with serpents and reptiles of various kinds and various numbers. St Anthony stood up and lifted his voice in Psalms saying: "Some put their trust in chariots and some in horses but we will be strong in the Name of the Lord our God." Immediately the creatures would disappear.

On another occasion, the devil came by night, holding torches of fire and saying: "We have come to burn you alive O Anthony!" Immediately, the saint closed his eyes and lifted his heart in prayer. The light of the evil ones was extinguished. A month later, they came back as singers of Psalms. They spoke with words of Scripture. Yet like a deaf man, St Anthony did not hearken to them at all.

The devils then shook down upon the habitation of St Anthony. The saint laughed at them due to his confidence in the Lord, and his mind was in no way disturbed. The devils came back whistling and beating their hands together but as soon as they saw the saint in Psalms, they lamented, wailed and beat their breasts in grief. Again, the devil appeared in a haughty and insolent appearance. The saint blew a puff of wind on him, and with the mention of Christ's Name, the appearance came to an end.

One time, while St Anthony was fasting, the crafty one appeared in the form of a brother monk carrying bread. He began to say to the saint: "Rise up, and satisfy your heart with bread and water. Rest a little from your excessive labors, for you are a man and you are clothed with a mortal body." St Anthony lifted his eyes in prayer saying: "O Lord, make an end of him as You have always done at all times." As the saint finished this prayer, the devil turned to dust and smoke.

Many times, the devil would appear in the form of a phantom which resembles gold. Singing songs of the Holy Spirit, our saint was never disturbed. Satan then laid cruel blows on the saint. The blows were multiplied yet the saint kept crying aloud saying: "There is nothing which shall separate me from the love of God." Hearing these words, the devil collapsed and vented wrath upon itself.

Satan approached St Anthony's dwelling again by night and knocked on the door. When the saint opened, he saw the form of an exceedingly tall and strong man. Having asked him: "Who are you?" He answered and said "I am Satan." The saint asked: "What do you seek?" Satan replied: "Why do monks revile me and why do they heap curses upon me?" Having clasped his head firmly in wonder, the Saint said: "Why do you give monks trouble? You know that Christ came into the world to pluck you from the earth and bring you to the lowest depths." As soon as Satan heard the name of Christ, he vanished and his words came to an end.

Let us not be frightened by these cunning phantoms. Let us not fear his impudence. Let us not be anxious from the evil one. Remember that God, who has exposed these powers, is with us at all times. If the evil one finds us submerged in the love of Christ, he has no dominion or power over us. Let us meditate on our Lord and let our souls rejoice in His hope. Behold, we shall find that evil vanishes from before us like darkness. Those who come to persecute us, will turn their backs on us like men who are chased out of battle.

THE BLESSINGS OF SAINT ANTHONY

The habitation of the monk is like a tabernacle of praise, psalm, hymn and spiritual song. Love and righteousness rejoiced therein and there is found a place of prayer, coupled with fasting. Monks toil in the labour of their hands and the sweat of their faces. "How fair are your habitations, O Jacob, and your tabernacles, O Israel!" The habitat of the monk is a paradise by the river, a tabernacle which the Lord had established and a cedar by the side of the stream.

St Anthony lived in his habitation and there he triumphed in the apparel of war. He despised the world and held it in contempt. His mind longed for the kingdom of God for he wished to be with the Lord. He used to say: "We should at all times follow the food of the soul, for the soul works together with our spirit in striving against the adversary. Yet it is right for the body to be in subjection and tribulation, for it very speedily becomes exalted by the persuasion and flattery of the evil. Therefore the soul should be more prepared and more exalted than the body, that the body may not prevail over it. Our Lord gave this indication to the blessed Apostles by saying, "Do not worry as to what you shall eat, or what you shall drink, for such things do the people of the earth seek after. Your Father knows the things you need so seek the kingdom of God and His glory, and the things which are superior to these shall be added to you."

The Persecution of Maximinus

Shortly after, a persecution arose in the Church, during the reign of Maximinus, the wicked Emperor. Soldiers began to seize a great number of confessors and take them to Alexandria. Report of this reached St Anthony. Straightaway, the saint left his habitation and made haste at the sound of the strife. He said to himself: "I will draw near to there, so if Divine Grace calls me, it shall find me prepared. If it thinks otherwise, concerning my unworthy self, I shall be a spectator of the strife."

St Anthony travelled into the city and inquired about where the holy athletes had been made to assemble. Upon meeting them, he became a companion to every one of them, ministered to them and relieved their wants. As they walked in, the saint gave them encouragement and admonition. As they came out, he ascribed blessings to them and sang hymns of praise. His acts became very popular among the city as news of the saint reached the governor. The wicked governor found out about St Anthony's disposition and work. He knew the saint was not moved by the tortures and tribulations that were befalling his companions. He commanded that the saint leave the city.

On another day, certain athletes were again summoned to the contest. St Anthony heard of the command and the threat of the judge so he washed and made white apparel with which he was clothed. Having arrayed himself with this clothing, he went and stood inside the hall of judgement, opposite the wicked judge. When the king's men saw St Anthony, they prevented him from appearing before the judge. Yet they marveled at his boldness and courage in facing death. God did not want the saint to face death at this time. God preserved the saint's life for the benefit of the monks, monasteries and the praise of the whole church. St Anthony headed back to his habitation, bearing witness and testimony continually.

ANTHONY DEPARTS TO THE INNER DESERT

On one occasion, a certain Roman nobleman whose name was Martinianus, came to visit St Anthony. He wanted the blessings and prayers of the saint because his daughter was torn by a devil. St Anthony looked out of his window, saw the nobleman and said: "O man, why do you weary me? I am a man like you. If you believe in Christ, depart in peace, and it shall be as you wish." Straightaway, the nobleman had full confidence in the word which he heard. Indeed, his daughter was delivered from the power of the devil.

Many people who were afflicted with diseases thronged St Anthony. As soon as they visited him, they obtained relief from their afflictions. When St Anthony saw that more and more people gathered around his cell, he became afraid lest he should be unduly exalted in his mind. He was determined in his mind to leave. He took some bread and sat by the side of the river, waiting for a boat. As he was waiting, the saint heard a voice from heaven saying: "Anthony, where are you going? Why are you departing from this place?" He was not afraid of the voice but he answered it saying: "My Lord, the people will not permit me to enjoy some silent contemplation. People are seeking that which is beyond my power." The voice again came to him saying: "If you want to enjoy silent contemplation, go to the innermost desert." The saint said: "O Lord, who will show me the way to this difficult place?" Now while he was standing up, there passed Arabs who were heading into that region. The blessed saint drew near them, entreated them to go with them for he knew this was a divine commandment.

Having travelled with them for three days and three nights, he arrived at a certain high mountain where he found water and palm trees. The place pleased St Anthony and he loved it well. The saint encamped there and was exalted like a king in the courts of his palace. The Arabs saw that St Anthony loved that place. From that time forward, everytime they would pass by, they would make sure to bring some bread for the saint in his dwelling. After a while, the saint walked around the mountain and found a place suitable for cultivating and watering. Thus, he began to provide for himself as much bread as was needed.

Once he started cultivating food for himself, some wild animals would come eat the crop. On one occasion, St Anthony caught one animal and said: "Why do you harm me, seeing that I do not harm you? Get going in the Name of the Lord, and never come again to this place." From that hour no wild animal harmed his crops again.

THE INEFFECTUAL ATTACKS OF SATAN
The blessed St Anthony lived alone in the desert and his mind was exalted and content. He was exceedingly old and far advanced in years. In

the desert, he endured strife, not with flesh and blood but with devils and impure spirits. The devils used to create sounds of tumult and outcry. They used to create flashing spears at night. The entire mountain would fill with fiery phantoms which would create great terror and havoc. However, the blessed Anthony was trained in stratagems of war. He stood up and rebuked evil. He was never afraid of visions such as these. He used to say to himself: "They are empty phantoms which perish at the Name of the Cross."

The saint was not terrified from devils, nor was he wearied by the desert. Satan suffered torture from all these things. One night, while the saint was standing in prayer, Satan gathered together all the wild beasts of the desert and brought them against him. There were so many animals in number. As the animals compassed him on every side, the saint looked at them and said: "If you have received power over me from the Lord, draw near and do not delay, for I am ready for you. But if you have come at the command of Satan, get back to your places and do not tarry, for I am a servant of Jesus the Conqueror." As soon as the saint said these words, Satan was driven away by the mention of the name of Christ.

On another day, the saint was weaving palm leaves. As he looked outside the door, he found an animal with the following form: It was like a man from its head to its side. Its legs and feet were like those of an ass. As soon as the saint saw this creature, he made the sign of the Cross and said: "How can the devil be so crafty. Devils are empty phantoms. Christ shall make an end of you. May you be destroyed immediately." Straightaway the creature started quaking and trembling. The creature ran away so fast that it fell down and burst asunder. The devils did all these things that they may drive St Anthony away from the desert.

VISITATION TO THE BRETHREN

Many monks began to beg St Anthony that he may come visit them. After multiple entreaties, he granted their request. He travelled with them in the desert, to the borders of Egypt. They had with them a camel which was laden with bread, water and provisions for the way. After two days of travelling, the water with them had finished for the heat was fierce in the desert and the monks were overcome by thirst. When St Anthony saw that the monks were in great distress, he sighed heavily and lifted his arms towards heaven saying: "Consider O Lord the prayer of your servant." Before the prayer was finished, water sprang from the place where he prayed. The monks drank and were relieved from their tribulations. Everyone filled their water-skins with water and thanked God.

They continued to journey until they passed by an inhabited village. People rushed forth to see St Anthony. He used to preach to all the people about true faith in Christ. He encouraged the village to preserve themselves from evil thoughts, the lusts of the body and vain boasting. He proclaimed prayer continuously as with the singing of Psalms. With such words, he would make strong and zealous the minds of all people.

St Anthony used to focus on the words of the Apostle: "Try one another and examine one another." He would encourage every man to make an account of his soul in works and thoughts, by day and by night. Every man is an honest investigator to himself, in front of Christ, the righteous Avenger, who rewards righteously and punishes justly. The saint would encourage those who fought against sin. He would admonish those who stood in truth and urge those with new exertions, lest they be stolen away by boasting.

Many who were smitten with sickness and evil spirits would come to St Anthony and the saint would comfort them with his words and aid them with his prayers. He encouraged those in sickness so they may not be disheartened in their tribulations. He made sure that those who were healed gave thanks to God alone.

The Wondrous Works of Anthony

One time, a certain nobleman went to the blessed St Anthony in the inner desert. This man was named Parniton and he was an officer in the palace. He had an evil spirit, gnawing his tongue and nearly losing sight to his eyes. This man went to St Anthony, entreating him to pray over him. Having done so, the saint said to the man: "Depart and you shall be healed." Parniton entreated him that he might remain with him for some days. The blessed Anthony would say: "You cannot be healed here. Go away from this place and when you arrive in Egypt, you will suddenly see the wonderful sign which God has prepared for you." Having confidence in these words, the man went away. Before he saw Egypt, deliverance came to him and he was healed.

There was a certain virgin of Busiris who suffered a severe and terrible disease. Her body was in a state of constant decay. Water was falling from her eyes and nostrils and her body was turning into worms. As a result of this disease, her eyes were losing power of natural sight. When the family of this young woman heard about St Anthony, they immediately went to visit him. St Anthony heard the story and said: "Go back to this maiden and you will find her wholly healed. This healing is not from me, but is a gift from the Redeemer who performs grace to all those who cry to him. Go back for God has heeded to your prayer and regarded the toil and labour of the family." When the family returned, the kinsfolk were rejoicing because the daughter was completely healed of her affliction.

Moreover, a certain Count called Archelaus

came to St Anthony and begged him on behalf of a nun called Polycratia. She was from the city of Laodicea and was faithful and devoted to the ascetic life. She was afflicted by pains in her stomach and her right side. Her whole body was suffering. When St Anthony prayed for her, Archelaus wrote down the day and hour in which the prayer had been made. Archelaus returned to his own country and when he had gone to the province of Laodicea, he found Polycratia in perfect health. Archelaus asked her at what time she had been healed. The exact time which Polycratia was healed was the exact same time which St Anthony had said the prayer. Numerous similar things had been performed on the hands of St Anthony.

On one occasion, St Anthony embarked on a boat to cross over a river. During the boat journey, a foul smell struck him suddenly. When the saint asked about the smell, the passengers on the boat said it is the smell of fish and salted meat with which the boat was loaded. Yet St Anthony did not believe this to be so. Suddenly, a young man with an unclean spirit was found in the boat. The devil abused the young man until St Anthony rebuked and silenced the evil spirit. Immediately, the young man felt deliverance. The foul smell was indeed the devil.

There came to St Anthony a well-known man who was tried by an unclean spirit. The man was so distressed in mind that his whole body was covered with lacerated spots and bites. The man with the unclean spirit approached St Anthony from the back and struck him. People began to rebuke the man but St Anthony said to them: "Do not be angry with him. This act is not of him but from the Evil One who is inside him." As soon as St Anthony said this, the young man was made whole and deliverance came to him. The young man began to salute St Anthony and confess the marvels of God with loud protestations.

THE DEPARTURE OF THE GREAT AMMON

When St Anthony was dwelling in the mountain, his mind was alert and watchful to observe and see operations of the Holy Spirit. On one occasion, he lifted his eyes and suddenly saw a man being taken up to heaven. The saint wondered greatly, magnified God and ascribed blessings to him who had been made worthy of this honour. Saint Anthony begged the Lord that he might know who the man was who had attained such exalted greatness. Suddenly a voice from heaven was heard, saying, "This is the soul of the blessed man Ammon who used to dwell in the country of Nitria." Ammon was a mighty man and a valiant fighter in the ascetic life. He had been a monk from his early manhood to his old age. The end of his life was greater than its beginning. It was a journey of thirteen days between the country of Nitria and the mountain where St Anthony lived. People marvelled that St Anthony knew about the departure of St Ammon. When they asked St Anthony how he knew, the saint said by means of revelation.

On one occasion, the blessed Ammon needed to cross a river called Dabha (Wolf River). With him, he had a righteous man called Theodore. When they came to cross the river, they agreed to meet each other on the other side. Theodore swam across the river. However, the divine grace seized Ammon and carried him across the river. When Theodore arrived on the other side of the bank, he drew near to the blessed Ammon, examined him attentively and found that his feet had not been dipped in the water and that not a drop of water had touched his body or his garments. Theodore began to entreat Ammon to see what had happened. Ammon did not want to reveal anything but when Theodore stayed persistent, Ammon told that he had been carried across the river by the Holy Spirit.

St Anthony and the Heretics
St Anthony was immeasurably firm in his faith and he held fast to honour and discernment. The Arian heretics were so detestable and contemptible in his sight that he withdrew himself from having any dealings with them. He exhorted other people to keep themselves far from their words and doctrines. At one time, some Arians went to St Anthony but he

drove them away from his presence like wild beasts and vipers. He said to them, "You are more bitter and more evil than beasts of prey and deadly serpents."

On another occasion, the Arians spread a report and made a scandal. They went about, saying, "Anthony has agreed to our faith and accepted it." When this report came to the saint's ears, he was astonished at the falsehood of the Arians and the impudence of their minds. When the bishops saw the wickedness of the Arians prevailing, they asked St Anthony to come down to the city to proclaim that these people are blasphemers. The saint came down and exhorted them in a loud voice saying: "Arianism is the essence of all heresies. It is the work of falsehood. Get away from them that you may not be corrupted by them. The Son of God is of substance with the Father and it is great wickedness for a man to say that there was ever a time when He was not. The Word existed at all times with God. Flee from association with them, lest you have a portion in their blasphemy. Light has no connection with darkness. You must have no connection whatsoever with them."

When an end was made to all these things in Alexandria, St Anthony departed back to the wilderness. As the saint reached the city gate, a woman came running and said: "Wait for me, O man of God. My daughter is grievously vexed by a devil and tormented. I beseech you to heal her." The blessed man looked up to heaven and cried out the Name of Christ over the devil. Straightway the damsel stood up and turned towards her mother. She was immediately freed from subjection to the devil. The saint continued in his journey to the desert. He was so happy to return to his solitude after a long absence.

The Wisdom of this World

Many people came to St Anthony, prepared to make a mock of him as if he was a fool. When the saint saw this, he said: "I will ask you a question. Which is older: Learning or the Mind? Which is the source of the other? Is learning the source of the mind, or the mind of learning?" The philosophers said to him, "The mind is the prince of learning for it has discovered learning." The saint said to them, "Does not then the man whose mind is enlightened surpass greatly him that has only learning? For by the first word he utters, they understand whether he possesses a wise mind or not." They marveled at what they had seen and heard, and they likewise went back to their own country.

St Anthony was a man whose intelligence was profound, wise and exceedingly understanding. When he became old, he was simple in his speech, austere and stern in mind, but still perfect and complete in everything. Every good quality was found in him. His speech was exceedingly savoury and well seasoned with heavenly salt, that none of his hearers could be angry at his words.

At one time, certain wise men came to question the saint about his faith. Having seen that they were ready to mock, the saint bore with them but roared greatly in his heart concerning the error that dwelt in them. He told them: "The religion which you preach is a service of impurity and desire of foul lusts. Christ is the Son of God and His Godhead was in no way changed. Through His care, He took Himself the body of our human nature. The coming of Christ took place for our redemption and it should not be a cause for fornication, falsehood, injustice, gluttony, drunkenness or lasciviousness. We exhort and admonish men to avoid these things for a penalty has been decreed for every man who practices this. Why do you make a mockery of the Cross and Resurrection? Why do you not recount miracles like the restoration of the sight of the blind, the cleansing of lepers, the healing of paralytics and the walking on waters? From these you can understand Christ and learn that he was not only a man but God also. Indeed, you appear to act unjustly. You give names to the earth, heavens, sun, moon, air, sea, fire, waters and to other created things. You call them gods, that you may lead man astray from the One God who is the Creator of the universe. What have you to say, O wise men?" When the wise men heard these words, they could not endure to hear from him any longer.

There was in that place certain men who were suffering injuries to their bodies. The blessed saint stood in their midst and said: "Let these afflicted souls have relief from their sufferings. Cease hostile attacks against Christianity and you shall straightway see the power of the Cross of Christ." The saint made the sign of the Cross over them three times and the people were healed immediately. The philosophers saw this and marveled greatly. St Anthony told them: "Why do you marvel at this? It is not I who have done this, but Christ who does these things in me." Such were the words spoken by St Anthony to the philosophers.

Esteemed by the Rulers of this World

The fame of St Anthony reached the king, the prince and Emperor Constantine. When his sons, Constantius and Constans, heard about St Anthony's works and triumphs, they began to write epistles to him so that the saint may pray for them. Whenever the saint received an imperial letter, he would gather the monks who happened to be with him and say: "You marvel that the kings and princes write epistles to us, but what need is there for wonder. You should wonder at how God wrote the Law for the children of men, and how He has spoken to us through His only Son."

When the saint replied to an epistle, he would first magnify those to whom it was addressed and return many thanks. He would encourage loving kindness among them, consideration to the poor and a reminder of the judgement of Christ which was to come.

One day, whilst the saint was weaving palm leaves, he fell in a state of profound shock. He saw a vision of revelation which made him groan and tremble. The saint began to bend his knees and pray with eyes full of tears. Those who saw St Anthony grew troubled. They began to press against the saint that he may tell of the vision he saw. The saint sighed and said: "It would be much better for me to die than for that which has appeared to me to happen. Great wrath is coming upon the church. It is about to be delivered to men who are no different to wild beasts. I have seen the altar surrounded by mules which have kicked all the people out. I have heard a voice which said: My altar shall be defiled."" Two years later, the trouble with the Arians took place and there was destruction of the churches by the hands of the pagans.

When the saint saw that this vision had disrupted the brethren, he consoled them and said: "My beloved sons, do not be afflicted for after these trials, peace will come upon the Church again. The horn of the righteous men shall be exalted. The time of these things is short and there shall be redemption for the people of God. The righteous shall live by faith."

Now the judges and governors entreated St Anthony to come back from the mountain.

This request was exceedingly hard for the saint so he excused himself from such a thing. The judges and governors saw that the saint refused what they had wanted so they dealt craftily with him. The saint was led by force back into the city. The saint would always say: "Just as fish die when they are lifted out of the water, so is the monk perverted and troubled when they are taken out of the wilderness." When the governor heard this, he marvelled and said: "Truly, this is a servant of God."

THE DEATH OF BALACIUS

There was a certain duke whose name was Balak (Balacius). He persecuted the church at the instigation of the Arians. His wickedness increased to the extent that he would beat nuns, strip monks naked and flog them. When St Anthony heard of this man, he wrote him a letter saying: "Behold, do not persecute the believers for the angel of wrath is coming." When Balacius read this letter, he laughed, spat on it and threw it away. Five days later, Balacius set out on a journey with Nestor, the prefect of Alexandria. They were both riding horses when suddenly the horse seized the thigh of Balacius and dragged him onto the floor. Three days later, Balacius died. Thus, the word of St Anthony came to pass and this laid wonder upon everyone that heard it.

St Anthony was accustomed to speak with the judges of this world. He would give them counsel in a loving manner and help them repent of their evil deeds. He looked after those who were treated unjustly. The saint's words were so grateful and pleasant that many people would forsake their life to become monks. Whoever came to St Anthony in suffering, would leave encouraged. Those who came with wrath, would leave long-suffering. Monks would come to him sorrowful in mind, yet would leave in great strength, ready for war. One monk came burning in lust. As soon as he saw St Anthony, the lust died inside of him. People from all over the world would come desiring to meet this saint.

CONCERNING HIS DEATH

St Anthony was one hundred and five years old and he knew the time of his departure. When the time drew near, his brethren wept bitterly. Each of them began to embrace and kiss him. The saint told them: "Do not despair over your tribulations. Do not lax in your works but be watchful as ever. Keep your souls pure from thoughts of iniquity. Strive for good gifts and guard yourself from heresies. Preach the truth of our Lord as you have been taught in Scriptures."

After a few months, the saint became sick. He cried to the brethren around him. There were only two in number. They had ministered to him since his old age. The saint said to them: "Behold, I go the way of my fathers. I am being called by my Lord. Take good heed that you remain strong in long-suffering. Increase it more and more and add to it each day. You are well acquainted by the wiles of the devil. You know their craftiness. Do not be terrified by them but always take refuge in Christ. Do not have any interactions with the Arians for you know how filthy their blasphemy is. Cleave to the Spirit of Christ. Meditate upon these things and keep them in your mind. Dig a grave and bury me in it. Hide my body under the earth and let my words be observed carefully by you. Do not tell any man where you have laid me. Divide my garments into lots and give one leather tunic to Bishop Athanasius. Give Bishop Serapion the other leather coat. Therefore, my children abide in peace for behold, Anthony brings his journey to an end and goes where Divine grace shall bring him."

When he had spoken these words, the brethren began to cry out and kiss him. St Anthony's face was full of unspeakable joy as he held his peace and died. The brethren did as they were commanded. They carried him out, dug a hole in the ground and buried his body in the earth. No man knew where he was buried except the two brethren.

Here ends the life of the blessed St Anthony. Old age did not reduce his vigour or compel him to gratify the body. He was not urged by the sickness of his body. God always preserved him from harm. Despite his old age, his eyes did not dim. None of his teeth dropped out. His hands and feet were in a sound and healthy state. He possessed strength which was not proportionate to his old body.

He did not become known to the world by means of his discourse, wisdom or crafty plans, but by his radiant righteousness towards God. Although these men of God live in secret places, God makes them shine like lamps upon all men. Let this little book be to every man a testament of a righteous father who left everything in pursuit of Christ. Our Lord honours those who honour him. He reveals his saints and proclaims their name abroad. Thus, is the story of St Anthony who triumphed in the contest and received the crown of victory.

Contemplations on
The Life of St Anthony
By Pope Shenouda III

PREFACE

Before I became a monk, the main field of my ministry was in the church of St Anthony, Shobra, Egypt.

When I left the monastic life for the ministry, I was invited by the church to give a talk about St Anthony, on the feast of St Anthony. This was 22 Tuba, end of January.

This book is the fruit of many lectures given in that church.

Shenouda III

Chapter 1
Our Love and Veneration
of the Saints

On the occasion of the feast of St Anthony, let us contemplate on the love of the church for its Saints. The Coptic Church has a great love for its saints. Large crowds gather to celebrate the feasts of St Mary, St George, St Anthony, St Demiana, Abba Ruis, St Bishoy, St Moses the black and St Maximus and Domadius. See the great love and veneration for the saints.

Saints have left this world, yet the world has not forgotten them. They are always present with us and we are always faithful to them. Although our fathers loved long ago, we continue to love them. This love is a deep seated virtue in our church. We love the fathers who have departed as well as those still living with us. We have great respect for their fatherhood, their life and their memory.

- John the Apostle says: "My little children, I am writing this to you so that you may not sin." (1 John 2:1)

- Paul the Apostle describes Timothy as "beloved child." (2 Timothy 1:2)

- He describes Titus as: My true child in the common faith." (Titus 1:4)

- He says to Philemon:" I appeal to you my child Onesimus whose father I have become in my imprisonment." (Phil 10)

- He says to the Galatians: "My little children in whom I am again in travail." (Galatians 1:4-19)

- To the Corinthians he says, "For I became a father in Christ Jesus through the gospel." (1 Corinthians 4:15)

- Also, St Peter says, "My son Mark." (1 Peter 5:13)

Thus, spiritual fatherhood has always existed in our church and we love our fathers.

A strong bond exists between us on earth and those in the world to come. "He is not God of the dead but of the living." We feel the saints amongst us and we talk with them as though they were alive. A person may stand before the icon of St Mary or St George and talk, or even complain. We always feel the presence of the saints and we always mention them in our prayers. St Anthony the Great is not only mentioned on his feast day, but in the liturgy and in the midnight prayer. We never forget our fathers since our church is characterised by fidelity and love to the fathers.

In honouring our fathers, we declare our belief in eternity. If we did not believe that St Anthony was interceding for us, we would not have celebrated his feast or sung hymns in his name. Are we honouring his dead remains? No, we are honouring the living saint. We believe his life continues into eternity and our lives will likewise.

In venerating the saints, we pay tribute to their virtues. Those who honour great scholars, show their respect for scholarship itself. Those who honour heroes, show their respect for heroism. Those who honour the intelligent, show respect for intelligence. Thus, those who love and honour the saints, honour and glorify the holiness in them. We love the saints because in their lives, there are qualities we love. The church in its veneration of the saints, pays tribute to these attributes of holiness.

In the lives of saints, we see religion practiced. We become confident that religious ideals are not just theory, but the road to perfection is attainable. The life of St Anthony teaches us many virtues. It illustrates that man can satisfy his needs from God. We learn how man can live in solitude and not feel lonely or bored. St Anthony's life is a real example of friendship with God. A friendship that fills the heart, the mind and the whole life. The Psalm says: "There is nothing on earth I desire besides thee." This is freedom from all material things, a true bond with the One. We see numerous practical virtues within the life of St Anthony: knowledge, discernment, humility, serenity and unity with God. We seldom see all these qualities in one person. Saints are excellent examples of what humans can be. Our love and veneration for St Anthony indicate our love for the life of prayer, contemplation, asceticism and monasticism. The admiration and love of the people for St Anthony are the reason for naming churches after him, painting his icons and celebrating his feast.

Our tribute to the saints is a tribute to God. God himself said: "Whoever honours you, honours me, and whoever accepts you, accepts me." We love God and love his children. Each calendar day has a saint feast. There is not a single day that does not carry memory of a saint. Saint feasts are assigned to the day of their death or martyrdom, since it is the day they completed their struggle on earth. The apostle says: "Consider the outcome of their life and imitate their faith." (Hebrew 13:7)

Everyone who lives a life of faith is a saint. St Paul writes: "To the saints who are at Ephesus and are faithful." (Eph 1:1) He also writes "to all the saints in Jesus Christ who are at Philippi." (Phil 1:1) St Paul closes his letter by "all the saints greet you." (Phil 4:22) He writes "to the saints at Colossae" (Col 1:2) and addresses the Hebrews by "holy brethren, who share in a heavenly call." (Heb 3:1) Anyone who has taken off the old nature and put on Christ through baptism, is a saint. However, here we talk about superior example saints, like St Anthony, who raised themselves spiritually, above the normal level. Saints like St Anthony strived long to reach high levels, proved their love to God and showed their readiness to live in unity with Christ.

Some saints were born saints and were even saints from their mother's womb like St John the Baptist who "will be filled with the Holy Spirit even from his mother's womb." (Luke 1:5) Likewise, Jeremiah the prophet, to whom God said "Before I formed you in the womb, I knew you, and before you were born, I consecrated you. I appointed you a prophet to the nations." (Jer 1:5) These are rare examples of the highest level of saints as that level of sanctity is a gift from the Lord. As for St Anthony, he was a youth, born to an ordinary but rich family. He strived and overcame great obstacles until he achieved victory.

Chapter 2
St Anthony Strived and Triumphed

St Anthony was not filled with the Holy Spirit in his mother's womb, like St John the Baptist. He was born an ordinary boy to a rich family. He was expected to inherit his father's wealth and marry. However, St Anthony strived to run away from all these assets. How did he achieve this?

He passed the test which Jesus set when he said: "It will be hard for a rich man to enter the kingdom of heaven; it is easier for a camel to go through the eye of a needle, than for a rich man to enter the kingdom of God. (Matt 19:23) St Anthony's reply was: "Lord, don't count me with the rich, for according to your commandments, I will sell all that I own, give it to the poor and follow you." Indeed, St Anthony possessed money, but money did not possess him. He never made money master him. When the demons scattered gold in the desert in front of him, it did not catch his attention, as though it was ordinary pebbles. Money had no value for St Anthony because his heart was saturated by God's love. Money is not dangerous, but it is dangerous to love money, yearn for it, pursue it, depend on it and brag about it.

Just as St Anthony conquered the love of money, he also conquered love of power and authority. He did not seek to keep his father's status.

He did not love the world as the commandment says "Do not love the world or the things in the world, for the world passes away and the lust of it." (1 John 2:15-17) St Anthony became pure in heart and lost all desire in the pleasures of the world. His heart became immune to the world and all that is in it.

St Anthony overcame love for his sister. He met his responsibilities for her by arranging for her support. He could have said: What can I do? I would like to live for God but I have family responsibilities. St Anthony loved his sister, yet he loved God more. He placed his sister in an orphanage and carved his way towards God.

At the beginning of his struggle, the demons attacked him with skepticism, yet he overcame them. The demons planted in his heart doubts about the righteousness of his approach. The demons tried to steer St Anthony away from the life of prayer and contemplation. They tried to make him worry about his sister and they burdened him with doubts, but St Anthony remained firm and nothing weakened his resolve.

Lack of guidance was another obstacle that St Anthony had to overcome. He lived in solitude and had no one to guide him. He had no church, no spiritual father, no help at all. He was able to do without all of these by taking advice from the ascetics who lived at the edge of the village. Later, when St Anthony lived in the mountains, he took his total guidance from God. God gave St Anthony wisdom and discernment, better than any other human guide.

In the barren and isolated desert, St Anthony fought and won the battle of fear. When the demons found that money, status and wealth had no value to St Anthony, they tried to frighten him. The demons appeared to him in the form of wild beasts, ready to devour and attack him. St Anthony conquered the fear in three ways: humility, understanding and prayer. Through humility, he addressed the demons: "You are strong. What do you want from me? I am too weak to fight the youngest of you." He also used to pray: "Lord, save me from those who think I am strong, when I am really dust and ashes." Whenever the demons heard such humble prayers, they disappeared in a puff of smoke. Through wisdom, he used to tell the demons: "I wonder why you gather against me in such large numbers. If you were really strong, just one of you would be enough." St Anthony knew deep in his heart that demons are weak and that through faith, he could scare them. The demons beat and tortured St Anthony, especially when he lived in a vacant tomb. St Anthony would recite the psalms: "The Lord is my light and my salvation, whom shall I fear? The Lord is the refuge of my life, of whom shall I be afraid. Though a host encamp against me, my heart shall not fear. Though war rises against me, I will be confident." In his deep faith, he used to tell his attackers: "If God gave you power over me, who am I to contradict God? If God gave you no power, then no one of you will hurt me." Thus, St Anthony lived a life of faith and courage. Every time he won a battle against evil, his faith grew stronger. St Anthony once said: "I do not fear God because I love him." This is the man who made the desert and mountains his home. The man who had no fear, even for the demons. Through his spiritual experience, he gathered his disciples and taught them that demons are so weak and no one should fear them. We can read this sermon in St Athanasius' biography of St Anthony. In all his greatness, St Anthony retained his humility. In one of his contemplations, he said he saw demons scattered all over the earth. He asked the Lord, "Who can escape this?" He heard a voice saying "The humble will."

One of the most practical examples of St

Anthony's humility, was listening to others without insisting on his own opinion. He was able to subdue his thoughts to others. Here are some examples of this...

+ He was committed to solitude. He practiced it by living enclosed for 30 years. He never saw a single human face. When people gathered around his door, asking for teachings, he never turned them away although he wanted to remain in solitude. He changed his way of life and began to teach monasticism, opening his door to all who wanted to visit. He changed his lifestyle for the sake of others and he accepted what God wanted him to do.

+ He believed monasticism meant abandoning the world and living in solitude in the desert. However, when the bishops asked him to go to Alexandria to fight Arianism, he went to the city and remained with the people for three days, until the mission was accomplished. Only then did he return to his solitude. He was obedient and did as he was told, although he was around 100 years old at the time.

+ Prior to that, he used to visit the martyrs awaiting trial and torture. He gave them his support and encouraged them. His modesty made him gentle and easy to deal with.

Due to his triumph over excessive asceticism, he was moderate in his style of life. He exercised wisdom and discernment with himself and others.

+ When St Anthony was asked about the most important virtue, he said: "Discernment which is understanding, sound judgement and wise action." He said that many who lived in the desert with prayers and fasting, still failed because they acted without discernment. St Anthony lived with wisdom and understanding, in contrast to other monks whose rigidity led them away, not just from principles of monasticism but also principles of spiritual life in general.

+ As a result of moderation, he conquered inner restlessness. He was cheerful. His face beamed with peace that his disciples liked to look at him. St Anthony triumphed over melancholy, that most monks thought to be part of monasticism. St Anthony was cheerful and kind. Although he lived in solitude, he greeted people with peace and love. He became an example of happiness and piety in a religious person. When you beheld his face, you saw peace, tranquility, cheerfulness and gentleness. He had the most comforting appearance.

Chapter 3
St Anthony as a Pioneer for a New Spiritual System

You have certainly heard of the many virtues that St Anthony had possessed. We do not know where to begin in talking about this great saint. I will discuss one of his most distinctive characteristics...his role as a pioneer. He opened a new road, a tough yet beautiful road, the road to monasticism. There were many monks at his time, but he was the one who established the lifestyle of monasticism. He was the first to introduce and explain the system. Pioneers in our religion have a steady place in our hearts. When we mention the divinity of Christ, we remember St Athanasius who fought against Arianism. When we mention the preaching of Christianity in the land of Egypt, we remember

St Mark who first preached the Gospel there. When we mention monasticism, we remember St Anthony who organised this lifestyle.

St Anthony started the road to monasticism. He was the father of a new discipline, a very tough discipline. This discipline is completed remuneration of the world and completed abandonment of all earthly things. When St Anthony started this road, he had no one to guide him. This is his greatness. Anyone who chooses the road to monasticism, will find many fathers to guide him. Guidance in the mysteries of this life, its depths, disciplines, and how to overcome the wiles of the demons.

However, St Anthony had no guide. He was on his own. The Bible says: "Two are better than one, for if they fall, one will lift up his fellow. But woe to him who is alone when he falls and has not another to lift him up." (Ecc 4:9-10) St Anthony was alone but he did not fall. He walked the road of monasticism without a father or guide. No companion, no man, no church, nothing to help him in the loneliness of the desert and his fight against the demons. St Anthony had complete faith that God was with him. He motivated himself as he walked the path of the unknown.

There are many books about monasticism that are authored by great fathers. There are biographies of fathers, ascetics and anchorites. Whoever does not have a guide, can learn from books. However, when St Anthony started, there were no books to learn from. He walked the path of perfection, without stumbling, because the Lord was guiding him.

St Anthony is not just a father to monks but to monasticism itself. He was the founder of monasticism and introduced it into the whole world. Whenever we want to know more about monasticism, we refer to St Anthony. This is why the life of St Anthony has an everlasting and wonderful effect. He gave the world a new plan for an order that was not known before. People used to come from all over the world to see this new life and how St Anthony made the mountains and desert his home. People were amazed because although St Anthony had not seen a man for 30 years, he was still happy through solitude and asceticism.

St Anthony was the wonder of his time. To look at him, was joy to the heart. One of his followers said: "It is enough for me to just look at your face, father." Many came to love monasticism through St Anthony. Many desired the same type of life for themselves. His silent life was a loud sermon that attracted many people to Christ. Monasticism became a new life, not just an escape from the world.

St Anthony was a wealthy young man with all the world open to him. He owned some of the most fertile land in Upper Egypt and his father was a man of great authority and status. He was the heir to his father's fortune and possessions. So why did St Anthony decide to leave the material world?

He did not flee the world, he rose above the world. This was the secret to his greatness and people's admiration for him. He grew above wealth, prestige and authority. He felt that the whole world was worthless. He taught all people to attend to their eternal life above all else.

St Anthony set up for the desert, leaving the world voluntarily. He gave up his fortune to live the life of poverty he chose. To live with God was an innovative approach to all people. It seemed unusual to live in a tomb. The demons tried to attack and frighten St Anthony but he always challenged their power by saying: "Unless God gives you power over me, none of you can harm me." The demons attacked him as lions and tigers but St Anthony stood his ground.

St Anthony rose and conquered fear, both in his tomb and solitude. He did not fear the demons, in fact, they feared him. St Anthony caught the admiration of people as he lived in mountains, amongst beasts and snakes, in fearful solitude, battling demons. He was never afraid and never succumbed to boredom. He lived so happily, preferring this life to worldly pleasures. He went into the desert armoured, not only with prayer and asceticism, but with courage.

St Anthony locked himself in a cave for thirty

years, without any visitors. People would come to his door, leave food and depart. Many people desired to live the life that St Anthony lived. A life of solitude, being content with God alone. St Anthony possessed so many high qualities. He was known for his modesty, knowledge, asceticism and spiritual wisdom. Others may have possessed some of these qualities but St Anthony outshined them all in pioneering the way to monasticism.

This great saint maintained his spirituality in great elevation and depth. An hour spent with God would support the church more than years of struggle in pastoral work. When Arianism threatened the church, St Athanasius fought it with verses from the Bible. He then called for St Anthony so that the Holy Spirit can work through his prayers.

Besides St Anthony, two other people concluded that the world was vain. The first was King Solomon who said "Behold all was vanity and striving after the wind and there was nothing to be gained under the sun." (Ecc 2:11) The second was St. Paul the apostle who said, "For his sake I have suffered the loss of all things, and count them as refuse, in order that I may gain Christ." (Phil 3:8) Despite that, St Paul stayed in the world to serve because he was held accountable for his work. He lived in the world but did not let the world live through him. Solomon remained King and Paul remained an Apostle. However, St Anthony did not stay in the world, not even for ministry. He went beyond the earthly rule of Solomon and the pastoral work of Paul.

Every monk in the world considers himself a son of St Anthony. Not only Coptics, but also Catholics and those of Eastern and Western Orthodox faiths. St Anthony offered the world a life of contemplation and prayer. A life of solitude, silence, asceticism and complete dedication to God. This solitude life offers no prestige, status, wealth or authority. Yet it offers greatness in the spiritual life, in the eyes of Christ.

Blessed be St Anthony who opened a heavenly door for us in the mountains. He blessed the sands of the desert. He pioneered the way of monasticism for us all.

Chapter 4
St Anthony as a Teacher and Student

Many have joined monasticism and become anchorites and saints, but none gained the fame of St Antony. St Anthony did not marry and had no biological sons, but he had thousands of spiritual sons in every country. All the monks in the world are his sons. When St Anthony enters the kingdom of heaven and says "Here I am and here are the children you gave me," thousands will follow him because he is the father of a new school.

St Ammon, the father of Mount Nitria, was one of St Anthony's disciples. St Anthony saw his soul ascending to the heavens, escorted by a joyous chorus of angels.

St Makarius the Great was instructed and given the monastic robe by St Anthony. He testified of St Anthony's greatness by saying: "A great power emanates from those two hands."

St Shishoy of the Eastern mountain, Paul the Simple, St Bisarion and St Sarapion were all disciples of St Anthony. So was Abba Bebnoda, Abbot of Fayoum monasteries, to whom St Anthony wrote his 20th letter.

St Hilarion who introduced monasticism into Syria and Palestine was St Anthony's disciple. St Anthony was the tree whose trunks and branches covered the whole world. St Anthony's followers did not only include monks, but one of the great popes of Alexandria. St Athanasius the Apostolic, the 20th Patriarch of Alexandria, was spiritually and theologically trained by St Anthony.

Christian scholars who study the theology of St Athanasius saw a reflection of St Anthony's theological ideas, an amazing correlation.

Many of St Anthony's disciples followed his footsteps through the biography written by Pope Athanasius, called "Anthony is life." This book helped spread monasticism in Rome and other western countries. Many people came to Egypt to be inspired by the life of St Anthony.

The biography of St Anthony left a lasting impression on St Augustine, such that he repented, became a monk, a saint and a source of contemplation for the world.

Wherever St Athanasius travelled in Europe, he

was asked about St Anthony. People longed to follow monasticism in Egypt as St Anthony left footprints in places he didn't even visit. People came from east and west to see St Anthony for advice. Philosophers visited him with questions and arguments. They were amazed at his great knowledge and intelligence. They questioned St Anthony saying: "You own and read no books. Where does your knowledge come from?" He used to answer saying: "What comes first, the mind or the knowledge? The mind! Thus, knowledge can be conceived by the mind, without books." St Anthony also told them: "When I wanted to know about something, I would pray to the Lord and he would reveal it to me. I meditate on verses from scripture and gain knowledge from there. I need no books." People came from all corners of the earth to seek one word of advice from St Anthony. They would take any advice from him as a guiding principle in their lives.

His fight against Arianism

St Anthony was a source of great holiness and a great teacher of spiritual matters. His words were words of truth and trust. When Arianism spread throughout Alexandria, the bishops told St Anthony to come and support the teachings of Pope Athanasius. St Anthony was over one hundred years old when he went to Alexandria. He stayed there for three days and implanted the true faith in people's hearts. Historians say that those three days had a great impact on the people. They were worth more than years of instruction. Every word that came out of St Anthony's mouth was supported by his holy life. He was God's man, speaking God's words.

When an ordinary man speaks, he needs evidence and proof to convince others of his argument. However, St Anthony was a man of miracles and wonders. He gained people's trust by his spirituality, needing to say only one word for people to believe him. St Anthony's word was the decisive word. Every word he said had its indelible weight.

St Anthony taught by word of mouth but also through his letters. He wrote twenty letters to his sons. They have been translated into Arabic manuscript and kept in monasteries. The last of his letters were to his disciple, Bebnoda. His letters have been published and studied by many scholars.

St Anthony had numerous teachings which were included in Palladius's Garden of Monks (The Lausiac History). It advises other monks concerning spiritual matters and asceticism. St Anthony's biography and life are a rich spiritual source.

St Anthony's biography, written by Pope Athanasius, includes a lengthy talk in which he discusses the weaknesses of demons. Demonic power is an illusion that people have. The biography explains that there is no need to fear demons. These words had a great impact on ordinary people, the elders and leaders of monasticism. St Anthony's words were a source of teachings and an impression of his face. One time, there were three monks who visited St Anthony to inquire about some matters. Two monks kept asking questions, while the third remained silent. St Anthony asked why he did not ask questions like the other two companions. The monk replied: "It suffices to look at your face, father." St Athanasius testified about St Anthony. "Whoever had a troubled heart or a bitter soul, will find people at once when he looks at St Anthony's face." St Anthony was a source of people to St Athanasius during his many troubles.

St Anthony loved discernment which comes from wisdom and knowledge. When one of his students asked about the biggest virtue in monasticism, St Anthony said, "Discernment. Many have fasted, yet hurt themselves. Many have prayed, yet failed. All due to a lack of discernment." One of his sermons in the "Garden of the Monks" addressed this issue. A person who acquires discernment can distinguish between the useful and the harmful, between the appropriate and the inappropriate. St Anthony emphasised this virtue and acquired it himself. He did not rejoice in sound opinions as much as he did in spiritual deeds. He once asked some visiting monks about the interpretation of a Bible verse. Each gave his own interpretation except Abba Joseph who remained silent. When St

Anthony asked why he remained silent, Abba Joseph said "Father, I really don't know." St Anthony replied "Blessed are you, because you knew how to say "I don't know."".

St Anthony as a Student of Learning

What sources of knowledge did St Anthony have? Where did he acquire his education? One cannot become a teacher, without being a student first. Where then did St Anthony study and who was his teacher?

St Anthony sought knowledge from every available source. That was his first quality as a student. He sought knowledge from everything and everybody, from every event, every person and even from every sinner.

He learnt his first lesson from a dead man. When his father died, he looked at his body and learnt something from it. His father owned 300 acres of the best farmland in upper Egypt. He had wealth, power and influence. St Anthony said: "Now where is this power, greatness and might? You have departed from this world without choice. I however, will leave it by choice." This was his first lesson about dying to the world. His father was a man full of power and influence, but now laid dead, motionless, without control over his own body.

St Anthony learnt his second lesson from the Bible. He used to listen to God's word in depth and he was a serious listener. He considered every word as though directed to him personally. One time, he was at church and he heard the Lord say to the rich young man: "If you want to be perfect, go sell your possessions, give to the poor and come follow me." The rich young man heard these words from Christ himself yet was saddened because the love of money possessed his heart. St Anthony heard the same words, and this made him literally go and sell all his possessions to the poor. St Anthony took the divine commandment seriously because he lived his life seriously. As he planned to depart from the world, he heard God's verse say: "Do not worry about tomorrow." Again he considered these words to be directed to him personally, so he hastened in escaping from the world.

In St Anthony's time, there was no monasticism as he was the founder of monasticism. How often do we hear these same verses read in our church, yet we are never moved to action like St Anthony was moved. St Anthony benefited from every Bible verse he heard as he put it all into practice. Bible verses were not just to be heard and enjoyed.

He was diligent in listening and transferring god's word into a way of life. He used to act according to the Lord's saying: "The words that I have spoken to you are spirit and life." he interpreted the spirit of the words and transferred them into a way of life.

Thus, St Anthony learnt his first lesson of

78   Contemplations on the Life of Anthony

monasticism from his dead father. Second lesson was from the Bible gospel verses. From where did he learn his third lesson?

He learnt his third lesson from good examples. There were a number of ascetics living on the outskirts of the village. He learnt something from each. Quietness from one, humility from another, silence from the third, continuous prayer from the fourth, asceticism from the fifth, keeping vigil from the sixth. He sought virtues from every person he encountered.

His fourth and greatest lesson was taught from a prostitute. One day while he was meditating by the River Nile, a woman came, started to undress, to bathe in the river. St Anthony reprimanded her saying: "Woman, aren't you ashamed of being naked in front of a monk." She replied: "If you were a monk, you would have gone into the mountain, far into the desert." The woman said this mockingly, but St Anthony took her words seriously and said: "Truly, God's word has come to me through this woman."

Thus, St Anthony left that place and went far into the mountains. His moving was a blessing to the entire world. He took the woman's demeaning and mocking words seriously. He considered them deep and spiritual. Many wicked women were great sources of blessings to the saints. As the Bible says: "Out of the strong came something sweet." (Judges 14:14) St Makarius the Great went to the wilderness as a result of a woman who had sinned with a man. She blamed St Makarius of this evil deed. She had a difficult labour and was on the verge of death. When she confessed her sin, people came to apologise to St Makarius for blaming him, but he fled from false glory, leaving the village and departing to the desert.

A sinful woman met St Ephraim, the Syrian, who was a very handsome young man. The sinful woman stared at his face for a long time. St Ephraim was embarrassed and reprimanded her. The woman answered him: "I am a woman and women were made out of man's rib so it is natural that I look at you. But you are a man who was made of dust, so you should look at the dust." He took her statement seriously and departed from her.

These women were not examples for us to follow but whoever is spiritual will benefit from anyone. They will use every resource to their advantage, even a sinful woman's words. The Bible says: "to the pure, all things are pure." (Titus 1:15)

We can draw spiritual lessons from the lilies of the field that are arrayed more splendidly than King Solomon in all his glory. We can draw lessons from the birds of heaven that neither sow or reap or gather into barns, but are fed by our heavenly father. We receive lessons from the seed and the sower, the wheat and the weeds, from nets and fishing, from yeast and from the prodigal son. He who has ears to hear, will hear what the spirit says to the churches.

One of our spiritual fathers has said: "I have learnt silence from the parrot. When I saw the emptiness of his talkativeness, I appreciated silence."

St Anthony learnt from meditating on the Bible. Our fault nowadays is that we read much and meditate little. Therefore we do not plumb the depth of our readings. St Anthony did not have many books as we do as he was a poor monk. He was not loaded with heavy manuscripts either. He used to read a little from the Bible and would not stop at the literal meaning of the words. He would dig deep into the spiritual depth of the passage. As St Paul the Apostle says: "I would rather speak five words with my mind, in order to instruct others, than ten thousand words in a tongue." (1 Corinthians 16:19)

St Anthony learnt from St Paul because his life was simple and pure, his conduct was exemplary. St Anthony learnt directly from God, through revelations and angels. When he was tempted by boredom, the Lord sent him an angel to show him how to pray and how to work with his hands. The angel showed him what a monk's uniform should be, with a head cover covered in crosses. When he was tempted by vainglory, the angel of the Lord led him to St Paul, the Hermit, that he might learn from his life and discover how to become humble.

St Anthony learnt from the devil's attacks as his

temptations were numerous and prolonged. He learnt the devil's tricks, thoughts, assaults and their attempts to have him fall into temptation. Through experience and practice, he grew strong and immune against these things.

St Anthony lived a life of solitude for more than eighty years. His life was filled with demonic attacks. They fought him with wicked thoughts, doubts and worries. They fought him through his senses and fearful visions. They attacked his chastity with visions of women. They appeared to him as tigers and lions and wild animals to frighten him, but St Anthony overcame them. They assaulted him by beating and tormenting. They left him on the verge of death. St Anthony would say: "The blows that rained upon me were so strong and severe, I doubt that any human force could hurt so painfully and cruelly."

When the boy that used to serve him found him in this coma condition, he carried him to the village church. The people saw him and wept for him. Around midnight, St Anthony opened his eyes and said: "Where am I?" When the boy told him that he was in the village church, St Anthony said: "Take me back to the tomb. Lock my door and go." St. Antony sat up and said to the devils, "If God has given you power over me, then who am I to contradict the will of God? If God has given you no power over me, then none of you can hurt me."

St Anthony then started to sing a psalm: "The

Lord is my light and my salvation, whom shall I fear? The Lord is the stronghold of my life, of whom shall I be afraid? When evildoers assail me, uttering slanders against me, my enemies and foes, they shall stumble and fall. Though a host encamp against me, my heart shall not fear. Though war rise against me, I will be confident."

Every time St Anthony would pray this psalm, the devils would vanish before him and disappear with a shout. The devils began to fear St Anthony, knowing that he was stronger.

St Anthony proved the power of the psalms and prayers, and the impotence of the devils when they heard them. St Anthony also learnt courage and firmness in his fight, gaining experience in his spiritual war and conflict.

St Anthony was a mighty man who lived alone in the mountains, filling the wilderness with prayers, meditations, praises, hymns, holiness and purity. The angels surrounded him from all sides, while the devils shook with fear. The saint's humility would burn every demon and drive it away.

On one occasion, Satan tried to wake up the saint from sleep for prayer. The saint was able to distinguish the devil's thoughts, tricks and dreams so he replied to Satan saying: "Whenever I want to get up for prayer, I will, but I will not hear the call for prayer from you." People were amazed at how St Anthony could recognise demons. The saint gained discernment and knowledge from his conflicts with the devils.

St Anthony taught others from the depths of his long experience. He never took up a book to explain his ideas to others. Rather, he lived, experimented, tested and taught.

He got to know the devils and their attacks; attacks through evil thoughts, through body, through visions and through dreams. On the other hand, he tasted the beauty of life with God; a life of solitude, prayers, consolation, divine revelation and meditation. He spoke to others out of experience, which is why his words were so effective. He had 90 years of experience. It was all a long journey with God, in the wilderness and the deserts, hand in hand with the Lord. He felt the heart of God and tasted how sweet the Lord is.

This great saint had his eyes open, discovering secrets, tearing down veils and seeing the unseen. On one occasion, his disciples saw him gazing up to heaven and sighing. When they asked him what had occurred, he said: "Today, a main pillar in monasticism has been removed. I see the soul of St Ammon ascending to the heavens, escorted by the angels." This bewildered the disciples. What did St Anthony see and how did he see it? Did he see it in the spirit or in his body? If it is in the spirit, then how could it be while he was still in the flesh? If it was by the body, then how could it be? Did the angels appear in a visible form? Did the soul of St. Ammon appear in the same way? Was he in the body, or outside the body? I do not know; only God knows. St Anthony was a clear eyed man to whom God unveiled matters and secrets.

The church is full of philosophers, intellectuals, priests, bishops and archbishops. Yet none as great as St Anthony. He despised the world and gave up everything in it in order to attain this great spiritual power. For him, GOD was everything. This saint excelled in spiritual matters as he experienced them, taught them and provided examples of them to others.

Chapter 5
Did St Anthony give or take?

There is no doubt that St Anthony gave to God everything that he possessed. He did according to the commandment: "He went and sold all he had and gave it to the poor." He gave to God 300 acres of the most fertile land in Bani-Seif. He gave to God his wealth, authority and all heirs of his father. He gave up marriage and all the children he could have had. He gave up a world of knowledge, science, pleasure and human relations.

This brings us to 2 questions. Did this saint give or take? Or did he give then take?

Does becoming a monk involve giving or taking? Is it a process of giving which then gets transferred into taking? Or is it a process of giving which then is rewarded by taking?

St Anthony gave up a 300 acre plot of land

but God gave him all of earth and heaven too. In every city, he now has monasteries, convents, churches and shrines. The whole wilderness became his because he is the father of monasticism. The land and property of St Anthony monastery in Egypt now exceeds what the saint would have given up in the small city of Kamn El-Arouss!

The Lord's promises never fail. "Truly I say to you, there is no one who has left house or brothers or sisters or father or mother or children or lands for my sake and for the gospel, who will not receive a hundredfold now in this time, and in the age to come, eternal life." (Mark 10:29)

When St Anthony gave up land to God, people must have thought: "Poor man, he has squandered his land, his wealth and his career." Yet God answers them saying: "He who loses his life for my sake will find it." (Matt 16:25)

The Bible says to St Anthony: "Lord your pound has made ten pounds more." (Luke 19:16) What did the saint give up other than land? Did he give up children? Suppose that young Anthony, instead of pursuing monastic life, had gotten married and had children. How many children could he have had? Five, ten, twenty? He now has thousands of monk sons in every generation that call him father. Millions of children from the beginning of monasticism and millions of children in the present time, spiritual children like me and you. Christ said:

"You will be compensated hundred fold." St Anthony was compensated thousand fold.

Christ even made St Anthony cross boundaries of time and space. The saint lived in the mountains, in solitude yet his name sounded in all corners of the world. All six continents of the earth know St Anthony. His name crossed the boundaries of his village, the frontiers of Egypt and the boundaries of Africa. He has children, monasteries and churches in every place. His shrines are also innumerable. Truly, did he give or take?

Sixteen centuries have passed since St. Antony's death, but he is still living among us. Living example of his principles, his teachings, his children and his memory. He is one of the eternal names that cannot be forgotten. His name was greater than death. Physical death could not put an end to his message. His life runs through many generations, having a beginning but no end.

When a monk is ordained, we pray the prayer of the dead over him, because he is dying to this world. Yet St Antony, by dying to the world, has entered a life that never ends, and through it he is still alive among us. Did he give his life to God or did he take a life that never ends?

Emperor Constantine sends to ask for St Anthony's blessings. Philosophers and noblemen come from all over the world seeking his wisdom. He attained fame like nobody else. For this reason the church calls him "St Anthony the Great."

What else did St Anthony give up for the sake of God? Did he give up priesthood? We are never told that he received an official post yet his sons because Popes and Bishops. St Athanasius the Apostolic was the Pope of this time and he was one of the spiritual sons of St Anthony. The Pope would kneel at the shrine of St Anthony and ask for blessings. If there were to be discovered a piece of cloth that proved to belong to St Anthony, all the popes, priests and people would vie for it.

Unfortunately, some people are reluctant to give. If the church asks a mother to give her son to the priesthood or the monastic life, she cries and falls sick as though a catastrophe is about to occur.

Among the mothers, I admire Saint Hanna, the mother of Samuel the Prophet. She could not conceive children and when God gave her Samuel, she gave him to God. After this, God gave her many other children whose names you may not remember. (1 Samuel 1:22)

Give to God and he will bless hundredfold, without you asking or waiting. Saint Anthony gave his life AND possessions to God. What happened next? God gave him a fertile earthly life, an eternal fruitful life and many children. The saint became a symbol. A symbol of life, solitude, meditation, prayer, virtue and spirituality. As the poet once said: "You are the symbol of a purified life which the creator desires to see."

He became a symbol of peace, tranquility. A symbol of a sublime life that only has time for God. A symbol against the world's trivial ties and ecstasies. Saint Anthony is a living example, a living picture, a living model. He is a letter read by all the people. In fact, an earthly angel.

St Anthony has given and God has ultimately given back. God gave the saint the power to be stoic, to overcome, to not fear. God gave him an amazing inner peace, a spiritual awe that filled the devils with fear. He was gifted with the power to take evil spirits out. Has this saint given or taken?

St Anthony left the joys of living in the world and instead retired to the loneliness of the desert for the Lord's sake. As a result, the Lord populated the wilderness with monks and turned the desert into a heaven. His cave became a shrine which people flocked to visit. His mountain became sacred. God certainly gives us more than he takes.

The spiritual man expresses his love to God through perpetual sacrifice and says to God: "And thy own have we given thee, O Christ." (1 Chron 29:14) The spiritual man feels the nothingness of his offering compared to what he receives from God.

For example, the story of Moses the Prophet. He left the palace of Pharaoh, refusing to be called the son of Pharaoh's daughter. He gave up all treasures of Egypt to become a shepherd in the wilderness. Do you think Moses lost or gained?

Moses gave up being a prince. The Lord now says to him: "I make you as God to Pharaoh." (Ex 7:1) We then see Pharaoh begging Moses to pray for him that God may lift his curse. It is evident that Moses was in a position stronger than Pharaoh's. Moses became the leader of the whole nation, a man of miracles who divided the sea and made water spring from a rock. There is no doubt that Moses has received more than he has given.

Our relationship with God is one of continuous taking, not giving. Do you think you give time to God in prayer? NO, rather you receive immeasurable blessings and gifts as the Holy Spirit works in you.

When St Anthony gave his life to God, it never occurred to him what he would receive in return. Feeling that we give God something is a spiritual mistake. Saint Anthony taught us that the spiritual life is a life of permanently taking from God. The taking of blessings and joy in every spiritual work.

From God, the saint took deep knowledge. A knowledge that the world could not give him. A knowledge that amazed philosophers and scientists of his age. Saint Anthony's words were all received from God. They had depth, strength and efficiency. God gave the saint "a mouth and wisdom." (Luke 21:15)

St Anthony's knowledge not only extended to ascetic matter but also theological matters. He silenced the Arians when he went to Alexandria. His words had the deepest effect on them. Scholars consider him as a teacher to Athanasius. When God puts a word in someone's mouth, He endows this word with a strength that no one can resist.

The saint was a good conduction device for the word of God, the gifts of God, the blessing of God and the peace that comes from God. Heavens were glad to find St Anthony who was a chosen vessel that could carry the blessings of God to all the people, without haughtiness or boasting.

God gave St Anthony the gift of miracles, great deeds and wonders. He healed the sick and drove away evil spirits. People approached him, not only for his spiritual knowledge but for his miracles. Does all this compare with what he gave up?

When the saint closed his eyes to money, God opened them to heavenly visions. An angel would appear to him and explain how to pray, how to work and how to resist boredom. Blessed are you St Anthony for your eyes that refused money began to see angels. Blessed are those ears that were dum to the songs of the world, but were found worthy to hear the voice of God.

Every time we give up something for God, we receive it double, without limits. He who refuses the treasures of the world will be opened to the treasures of heaven. St Anthony gave up marriage but saw the sweetness of his sons. Among his sons were St Makarius (the father of Skeet), St Ammon (the father of Mt Nitria), St Bebnoda (the head of the Fayoum monasteries), St Hilarion (the founder of monasticism in Syria and Palestine), St Paul the Simple, Fr Bisarion, Fr Sarapion, Fr Shishoy and many more.

Truly, "Sing Oh barren one, who did not bear; break forth into singing and cry aloud, you who have not been in travail! For the children of the desolate one will be more than the children of her that is married, says the Lord." (Isaiah 54:1)

St Anthony gave his whole life as a sacrifice to God. God took it, sanctified it, blessed it, enhanced it and gave it back to the world. God says: "My son, give me your heart." (Proverbs 23:26) The Lord wants to take your heart to fill it with love, blessings and goodness. He wants to take your heart and purify it from every sin. When you give your life to God, you are giving him your emptiness so that He can fill it. You are giving your weakness and taking God's strength. "The windows of heaven will be opened to him and God will pour down blessings on him until he cries: Enough!" (Malachi 3:10)

Advance towards God. Give Him your will so that He can give you back strength and victory. Are you then giving or taking?

Chapter 6
St Anthony and the Love of Solitude

St Athanasius the Apostolic reported that St Anthony enclosed himself in complete solitude and did not see a human face for 30 years. He experienced the fruits of quietness while he was in solitude with God. He would empty his mind from worldly news and trivialities, to fill it with God alone.

St Anthony tasted the sweetness of solitude so he used to say" "The monk in the monastery is like a fish in the sea. He cannot survive outside of it."

After St Paul the Simple lived with St Anthony for a few years, St Anthony told him to go into the wilderness, to live in solitude, to "test the assaults of evil." He would always say: "Sit in your cave and the cave will teach you everything."

St Anthony would engrave into every monk the love of silence and solitude. He would kill the world in every monk through quietness. Saint Isaiah says: "Just the sight of the cave kills from the heart all worldly moves."

Moses was trained in the wilderness, more than he was educated by the Egyptians. God drove Abraham to the wilderness where he was trained in a life of tents and sacrifice. This is estrangement from the world and the sharing of life alone with God. Elijah trained in the wilderness on Mount Carmel. John the Baptist also trained in the wilderness. Our Lord Jesus Christ lived in the wilderness on the Mount of Olives where he spent the night in prayer. (John 8:1)

Likewise, St Anthony lived, not just for a few days but for his entire life. He lived away from the city and its noise and glamour. He lived away from the worries of the world that tangle people and prevent them from enjoying a life with God. Every mountain, wilderness and desert represents solitude, away from the tumults of the city.

Our Lord Jesus used to take his pupils to the wilderness where they can concentrate on his words, without being preoccupied by other thoughts and sights. Every person in this world needs to spend times of retreat and quietness with God alone. In these moments of retreat, one can examine themselves and enter into a special depth with Christ. This life of quietness and retreat has numerous spiritual implications.

To live in the wilderness, requires special motives. The first quality is asceticism. He who loves the world is attracted by worldly matters and cannot stay long in the desert because the world is too dear for him. The Gospel says: "For where your treasure is, there your heart will be also." (Matt 6:21) Only the person who has truly died to the world, can live in the desert.

Death to the world is a definite prerequisite of life in the wilderness. St Anthony's heart had died to the world and all its desires. He left his people, his town, his money, his power, his everything. He no longer desired anything worldly. This is why he could live in a cave and bear hunger, thirst and solitude.

Living in the wilderness also requires a courage of heart. It requires a heart with no fear, that is not afraid of solitude, darkness, wild animals, beasts or devils. St Anthony had very frightening attacks. The devils would appear to him in the shape of fierce animals. They would cry with fearful voices and attack him. Even then, St Anthony did not fear but stood solidly, facing them. The devils would attack brutally yet St Anthony was not shaken. Later, the devils began to fear St Anthony and he attained the power to drive them away.

St Anthony was the man of the wilderness, the son of the mountains, the man with a fearless heart. He lived in the desert with only God keeping him company.

Living in the wilderness requires one who can spend his time well, lest he be bored by the emptiness that surrounds him. Solitude is a positive attitude in life with God. Clinging to Christ, tasting his sweetness and company with Him.

St Anthony lived a life of prayer and a life of meditation. Solitude became a spiritual pleasure for him due to the divine company that filled his life. He did not live alone in the wilderness but God was with him. He knew that "Only One is needful" and he succeeded in being attached to that One. Saint Isaiah says: "With the quietness of the body, we acquire the quietness of the soul."

St Anthony's senses, thoughts and interior heart became calm. All his features were repose. He became a source of peace for all those who came in contact with him. People loved his calm, quiet life which was filled with peace. The purity of his thoughts increased little by little until there was only God in his thoughts. All worldly matters were erased from his mind for there was no use of them. His mind was only rooted in divine matters. His life became concentrated in God, including his thoughts, feelings and words. The world died around him and in him.

As for you my brothers and sisters, if you cannot live in the mountains, do not deprive yourself of some solitude and quietness. Even if it is for a few days per year or a day each week or an hour each day. Shake off the tumult of this world and sit with God, accepting His aid. Do not spend too much time amidst the worries of this world but withdraw yourself. Be like strangers on this earth and think of God and his kingdom. The important thing is to have the love of quietness in your heart.

My advice to you is: Do not let worldly matters enter the depths of your thoughts and feelings. Do not let the world settle in you and dominate your mind. St Anthony's life was characterised by his love of solitude. He was in love with God. He was not being an introvert, hating people and unable to deal with them. It was solely solitude for Christ, filled with goodness and gentleness.

Chapter 7
St Anthony and the Love of God

When the love of God reigned in St Anthony's heart, fear was completely eradicated from it, even the fear of God. Hence his famous saying: "My sons, I do not fear God." When people heard this statement, they said: "This is hard to say, Father." But St Anthony would say: "This is because I love Him and love casts out fear."

The spiritual life begins with the fear of God as the Bible says: "The fear of the Lord is the beginning of wisdom." (Proverbs 9:10) Once you experience the spiritual life, you find joy and ecstasy! Fear disappears and love remains. As one grows in his love to God, "Perfect love casts out fear."

Without St Anthony's love for God, he could not have lived in solitude. The love of God is a crucial character in one selecting solitude. We say in the distillation prayer: "and they lived in the mountains, in the wildernesses and in the canyons of the earth, for the sake of their great love to Christ, their King." It is love that motivated fathers, monks and anchorites to live in the mountains.

For the sake of this love, our saint gave up everything. For him, God was more valuable than anyone or anything else. He needed no other love for comfort and support.

The love of God is the motive for solitude and prayer. St Anthony loved God and because of this, he wanted to be alone with God. He could not bear to part with him. As the spiritual elder says: "The love of God estranged me from humans and from human matters." The saint found pleasure in addressing Christ as David the Prophet says: "Beloved is your name, my God. It is my recital all day long."We also say in the Praise: "Your name is sweet and blessed in the mouth of your saints."

How beautiful is the saying of David the Prophet: "For me, it is good to be near God." (Psalm 73) How can one abide in God if he is too busy with the feelings and thoughts of the world.

Whoever tastes the love of God, finds everything else to be trivial. The sweetness of God makes everything else lose its meaning and become vain and futile. St Paul says: "I count everything as loss because of the surpassing won of knowing Christ Jesus my Lord." (Phil 3:8)

Asceticism is not the act of forcing one's self to leave the riches of the world. Rather, it is a deep conviction of the triviality of everything. This conviction is the result of love for God. When one sees that all the pleasures of the world do not satisfy him, he gives them up because his heart has been opened by a greater love. The love of God is deeper and more sublime, causing everything around it to dwindle and diminish. On the other hand, any worldly love will eradicate love of God from one's heart. The Apostle says: "The love of the world is enmity to God."

We ask ourselves: How could St Anthony live alone in this distant cave? How could he bear the lack of human consolation? How did he find fulfilment in his solitude? The answer is: He was filled with the love of God and hence needed nothing else. Living alone was not a solitude for him, it was rather a life with God and his angels. A life sweeter than life with humans and society.

A hymn by HH Pope Shenouda III to the Great Abba Anthony

In the Church of the firstborn
In the pure assembly
Living in all piety
PENIOT ABBA ANTONIOS

You are in a glorious state
Among those of the Eskeem
In the rite of the Seraphim
PENIOT ABBA ANTHONY

With spiritual prayers
Living a godly life
You consecrated the desert
PENIOT ABBA ANTHONY

With struggles in prayers
For many decades
And tears in the metanias
PENIOT ABBA ANTHONY

In ascetic fasts
For days at a time
With an unfailing spirit
PENIOT ABBA ANTHONY

With meagerness in pleasures
Concerned in godly matters
And spiritual meditations
PENIOT ABBA ANTHONY

You were given the spirit of Elijah
And Hannah the prophetess
And John, the son of Zacharias
PENIOT ABBA ANTHONY

The devils feared you
Because of your upright heart
And your constant prayers
PENIOT ABBA ANTHONY

They fought against you daily
They tried every possible way
Using many tricks
PENIOT ABBA ANTHONY

They reminded you of yoru sister
In order to worry you
So you might return to the world
PENIOT ABBA ANTHONY

They scattered gold and silver
Before you on the mountains
Glittering in the midst of the sand
PENIOT ABBA ANTHONY

They came with chants and songs
And images of women
To make you fall into temptation
PENIOT ABBA ANTHONY

They came with fierce visions
Of lions, tigers and leapords
And with sounds of thunder
PENIOT ABBA ANTHONY

They came with their malice
So you might fear their visions
Your humility disgraced them
PENIOT ABBA ANTHONY

You proclaimed and said to them
"O you strong ones
I am but dust and sand"
PENIOT ABBA ANTHONY

"I am surprised at your gathering
And swarming on my weakness
I am weaker than your weakest"
PENIOT ABBA ANTHONY

O strong and high tower
An example for the meek
Humble even before Satan!
PENIOT ABBA ANTHONY

You are a powerful example
Throughout the generations
O dweller of the mountains
PENIOT ABBA ANTHONY

Your life is more than light
It is a fragrance of incense
It is to be sung like a psalm
PENIOT ABBA ANTHONY

You are great in struggles
O the wise in counsels
Pray on behalf of your children
PENIOT ABBA ANTHONY

We have not practiced your life
Nor acquired your likeness
Remember us in your prayers
PENIOT ABBA ANTHONY

Pray for our iniquities
And the weakness of our nature
For we are strangers in this world
PENIOT ABBA ANTHONY

www.ingramcontent.com/pod-product-compliance
Lightning Source LLC
Chambersburg PA
CBHW051734040426
42447CB00008B/1127